HÍVADO

HÍVADO

ANDREW E. COLARUSSO

Flood Editions, Chicago

Published by Flood Editions

www.floodeditions.com

ISBN 978-1-7332734-9-7

The author wishes to thank Forrest Gander,
Don Ramón Rivera, Devin Johnston,
and Josue Agosto Rodriguez, quien desde
pequeño me ha dado luz en la oscuridad.

Portions of this book appeared
in *Almost Island* and *Callaloo*.

Design and composition by Crisis

Printed in Michigan on
acid-free, recycled paper

For Josue Agosto Rodriguez

and Sebella Rose

HÍVADO

gun to my chest heavy with the weight of
what hasn t happened yet   I fell

asleep   with a noose around my neck
ground glass in my palms-   -and a razor

in my sex-   -under my tongue
I m sorry-   -there is no happiness

there is no pleasure-   -nothing is left
and I can t wait-   to tell you about it

I sat there-   -watching
from a tall wooden stool-   as fold by fold

behind the counter   -she built boxes
studying my slouch   for a cabinetry

crafted   from the stillness of my mouth
which held her morning   after

morning thereafter when still-   -dark
in water so hot it peels away from-   itself

as though   she had been
ungiven   clutching her narrow knees

to her chest-   -yellow her underthigh
lowered-   -her eyes pressed hoarstill on

her own bed its-   -blankets fixed
surface-   -yellow to her underside

watching a small set   -its bluing light
over a graven image-   of the virgin mary

to the window taps the   graygreen
grass of the cerro-   in glass

warped-   panes wet with mist its
paint chippt and   muntins effloresced

beneath it a small table   in the georgian
made of mahogany   imperfectly finisht

but by hand   on top of which sits
four plum stones- -a plate of dry lavender

I ve seen-   -through you
my body-   transgressive

vault of what not-   -society shall become
from stalks of black   lamping even

-ingrain   smoke over-rails
an authority on   repeated phrases like

you are the animal-   -asking to learn
but I won t teach you-   how to cat daddy

when a flapping of wings   by sound
alone makes presence known- -she wakes

in the middle of-   what from her belly is
misst-   moaning I want-

beating against the floodgate-   -an egret
carrying an eye   humming in the cold

downbourn of a cataract   and jingle
unborn in the brush   of berries perfumed

there are ghosts   -forming while
sitting in a room-   with people who all

they have for you-   in accordance with
the laws of god and   man are

-questions they want what   -darkness
hobbled within you   for soft science

and through this   the consciousness
of fog-   -assumes creation of the fogged

abrades clarity   of the palm
in the scorn of strangers   -and the starved

flayed   -you are neither
to have his baby   -nor will you be free

from the depths   of this fog
you will not find your nest or the memory

of never having had a nest   -you remain
and listen to a flapping   as the creek rise

outside things do moan   bottled desire
but only in the light   -and quietly

the lives of birds-   affirmed
a world of spirits-   -on the b side

I saw a pigeon   with a broken wing
huddled-   -under the architrave

outside-   -of a chiropractor s office
staring into the glass waiting for a healing

I sat there-   -watching
as jets taxi d televisually   from the tarmac

vibration   like gravel passing
through plate glass and-   through steel

I thought of what I d left   left
in limaní where   -before leaving

she undressed at the mouth of   el charco
piling her clothes on a stone-   she paused

at the firm lip of el charco-   waiting bare
as I undress-   -she turns to face the falls

beneath the gaze of a darner   -I undress
unbuttoning   -one hundred chinos

one hundred times-   -still soft and
unlading my dense head-   -hit with heat

one hundred times   the burnished river
stone-   -retracting then coated in cool silt

between my thighs   waiting bare
the river sediment--pressing into the flesh

of her heels- -which when shifting weight
lit with blood and   tore some

unpeeling dead skin at the lip of el charco
hands   at her sides palms open and wet

with patience   sweat like mercury down
the split of her back   -I take off my socks

I shift my full body s weight   -fallward
onto the balls of my bare feet-   -sediment

pressed unfamiliar   -one hundred times
the irony of character in notable hermetic

lives   lived cleanly and finally
by ferule   one hundred times exciting

my plantar nerves   to a threshold
of pleasure-   -accumulating a sort of pain

I am one hundred times-   -the earth
departing a darner in flight-   -and one

approaching a woman   waiting at the lip
of el charco-   -what is it you want

to know-   -about this woman
her hair where it grows   or the shape of

her intuition-   -her skin how it can carry
the full light of a sun   -she stretches

el charco   where it meets her heel
swallows its dead skin   she runs

her left hand down her side-   -and signs
with her walking drawl-   -no temperature

where el charco meets her ankles-   -and
rippling climbs her thigh until-   -her lips

beyond the lip of el charco   -have parted
she waits afloat-   -in the belly of el charco

because-   there is no spume
my skin knows-   -with such familiarity

submerged-   in the blue green depth
my mouth held in-   the birch bark of

her palm held the weightless mass of   my
lingering beneath the mercury-   -head

of el charco her lips-   -warbling above and
bellow widely   with all of her great loves

I hear her   one hundred times amplified
in the cool belly of el charco   -calling

I know the break   in her clavicle
the molar distortion   -that colors

her chords above   my beryl chamber
a sound without reproach   and

softens the lip of my machine   -what I left
left in limaní-   arrives with my flight

I sat there-   watching
as with his fingers-   -he set upon

his scalp   fixing his filed thumbnail
into a dorsal pole between two tight curls

until a crack a calcitic- -crack not of bone
splintering   but nerve snapping

at a southbound terminal-   made me
at his severed commissure   -blink twice

he at   the station spilled light from
the space held forth   -an opened crown

and wept for   some time before its arrival
the height from   which he fell falls must

from the chill glim   -his head gath
ering dust   -and the remnant carcasses

from a colony-   -stranded after winter
four strung up   -from a spider s skein

black bodies-   -hanged in the gas heat
beneath the radiator-   -where he lay

his head-   no longer weeping
he gets up to nod-   once in a while

though he cannot stay   cannot say

the station is   -filled
around him lulled   with sentient stories

when I close my eyes   -I see capillaries
I see light from inside   the terminal

the bus has arrived   -no one notices him
but   the din of life surrounds him-

someone points-   -to the bus
in the glass above him   -that one that one

那個 那個

let me see you   let me go
look at you all grown- she said to her boy

wearing a victor cruz jersey   -flanked
on his right   -by his much taller father

she held his cheek   -warming her palm
then kisst his nose-   she said to her boy

football players don t cry i ll see you soon
my son-   then she got on the bus

her laughter went off-   -like a cymbal
from the pri v   a solitary sort

ilege shivering   of laughter that woke
the sleepy imagination of   the bus driver

a mother of four-   -and a murmuration
floating up-   -through the coach

from the back of the bus-   making stops
at ears tuned   to petty curiosities

she laughed-   for the rest of the trip
in soft spasms-   approaching sobs

upon arrival   -I hailed a cab and asked
the driver-   -if he d take me to brooklyn

kobina was his name   -my man tuesday
said yea sure whereto- -asked wherethere

this doesn t never happen   not nowhere
for negus like me   I won t carry you

common but na today- -down these rues
so many pretty redheads out--said kobina

before we reached the bridge   before
I fell asleep dreaming of-   auburndark

hair fallen   -in the audubon ballroom
I realized   she was crying

on the bus   and
I couldn t tell you   why

I sat there-   -watching
in the backseat-   the familiar ingress for

it s emenan t-   all noise
coming   from the brownstone

which once stood as would- -a pipe organ
loudly along the avenue-   -of my boyhood

where was the radio-   a way of breathing
is now a mendicant-   -muttering alone

the smell of it settled   -in the brick
and the paint on the crown a   dull brown

pity for the sinner he said   to the tune
of a rook obscured- of a robin redshifting

and the mourning dove   -omnisonant
in that order-   -along a black fence

I don t understand-   it s simple he said
she don t live here no more   she gone

                              just let me in   just let me up

there is slowly-   -pluto passing through
the lion of   a dogsbody

lightening at the fore-   withclosed
from some young girl moaning   -out the

wide-   third floor window
and as pale as the sound   which is ofcome

is gone deep-   over the beak of a tawny
to sleep   where I ve happened to you

I sat there-   watching
in tall earth   while a red breast

with worm half in shadow   stood idle
beneath a birch in full bloom-   and why

trembling I felt my pulse-   -rise
and clutch at my skinn-   touch it my sing

ed neck stung   under light passing
through-   its black mandibles upon me

I pulled it from my neck   still raging
still flailing-   -at my presence

obsidian and muscular   pulled so quickly
and with such alarm   it must ve been

torn apart from its mandibles left pulsing
in the muscles of my throat   on the paper

I threw it-   toothless and on fire
before crushing it-   -under my thumb

its body left a residual music   -nerve
snapping its legs and antennae- -ticking

in a way I could no longer describe   as
anxious maybe and-   -the bird

disturbed   flew away
I was left   -with the boy s bleeding mouth

I was left   with atonal music and
a generation   with no regard

for low flight-   -come screaming
across the skyline-   I could see it

bleeding against pluto- -from her window
on the day   -now I am here

where the purging is impersonal   where
penderecki is left   to play on a loop

in every languid parlor and   is heaving
she no longer lives here-   -and

the earth beneath me is   -disquieted
shifting anxiously   -when I think of her

space now occupied by a   -nonce noise
child of white flight   -which vacates me

trembling   -and every lie that I am
trying   -to explain an absence

to justify the disrepair   that comes with
a decaying   -memory

a sparrow   fanning itself with dust
whips up a quick cloud   -diffracting light

that carries   increasingly diffuse
across memory lane-   -sitting in the park

I am left   to consider apostasy

a procession of ants pass not-   -pausing
to collect from the paper-   -the remains

and so acknowledge-   -this one of
the colony as lost   a willed divestment

do they whisper-   -among themselves
when carrying   -the noble dead

inches   beneath the surface of the earth
the largest of them   carrying a sugarcube

Jun 12,

c/o: RA

             is to dream   -constantly overturning
             tables-   -the south fate called for

             carved ivory   the stock against
             my shoulder   a moon clip in my mouth

             beneath the surface-   -was no witness
             to bare affirmation   that what we had

             experienced and then   lived through
             was uncanny   -became color redress

if a black door   -behind me I speak
which reward it was-   the dream

dream-   of the amorous
mouth to back-   -turned to catch

what residual steam it is that   funnels
upward from your body   of its sudor

evaporates   then I will not thispare
I have every-   intention

free and easy   for the closed mouth
of the keyed-   -his scherzo

sounds   in the close mouth
of the receiver-   -can you tell me please

who won-   -what wooden ships go sailing
who are you-   -playing

I am listening now   -though it is late
for these cadences   -of our peregrination

I sat there-   -watching
as wind-   fanned flame in a steel drum

began   the construction of my obstacle
from the hilt   -a sheaf of his dated letters

on which I lay my temple   -in faint light
in feint-   what cannot be seen

is drawn a series of his mediations- -from
a lost ledger and   -redistribution

there I slept-   -there I would work

begins the ritual rite   the agonist must

in the glow-   -as dark settles in the park

red

its boreal music	-moves with eve
between-	-the bloodcolor
foliage of a young maple-	-sap
hard for the sugar house-	ambering
over	a thin rachis
the clapboard	still warm to touch
alarmed in mars-	makes promise
departing	-to leave the light on

green

red handed   -tonic
in a bed of bees   -scaling

prints to cast-   -copper sheets
past registers   in rough hewn forms

of dispute settled as   a layer of dust
thin and hoary-   -over its eaves

inflorescence   flowering
in the casement   ineloquent silence

blue

in them a dulling-   -for the verdure
that was once-   -an elasticity of limb

the carnation slip   shrinking the wide
of its golden iris-   indifference

in dusk   from the vane of the hovel
hanged-   -high in the barer hinterland

that human hand   embowered
in shadow holding-   -its once verdure

cyan

hanged high-   -in the barer hinterland
embowered in shadow   holding

red handed   in difference
over its eaves-   -the carnation slip

that was once   flowering
thin and hoary-   in the casement

shrinking the wide-   -past registers
of dispute   -settled as a layer of dust

magenta

in them a dulling   -in dusk
makes promise-   -the bloodcolor

of its golden iris-   ambering
over   -its boreal music

an elasticity of limb-   -moves with eve
embowered in shadow-   -holding

high in the barer hinterland   between
the carnation slip   still warm to touch

yellow

flowering   -foliage of a young maple
a thin rachis-   alarmed in mars

makes promise-   -over its eaves
to leave the light on   -red handed

in the casement-   -still warm to touch
hard for the sugar house -in a bed of bees

its boreal music   -thin and hoary
tonic-   -in eloquent silence

white

this is the conquered world-   at sundown
pinkly dusted   soughing

a song-   -the yellow back wet
sloughed off   -staring down

over the self   -involved limbs
of the taiga   into an ether of geese

and the sound of them-   that chaste me I
is not like you   -I cannot be talked down

no a sus lavios   musica
derrompiendo la sombra   pero acostao

en las corrientes de la ciudad-   el cuerpo
despierta-   -resinoso

oliendo de crica-   y devenustando
en cuya casa-   -el grajo

fumando y   -de una masa
brumoso-   -espeso y omnitranquilo

hums an invocation to rend the integrities
under the dark canopy-   -of the natural

hemmed in by   heat cast from
the mendicant meal where   beyond

the trees are recognizable-   -no bodies
to drape the abyssal   in sacrifice

the walls of the obstacle   on which I build
my aggravated sleep   -from red eyes

doggedly observe   the worm that moves
not to meet   -the body

but earth that   parting from the agonist
consumes the body-   -consuming itself

it forms its natural shape   tall and rusted
with   an opening at center for the body

drawn from the agonist its limbs hanging
hungry for whose-   -knuckles

as the sentient edifice rears-   blowingly
back among the weeds-   it grows

its own light foehn-   -fugal from
its fulminant girding   where lay pity

to sate the appetite-   for the colossal
and its entropic   generation of language

tusks in the dark   jutting through fire
where cinders line the heavy path   to slip

contracting and   expanding
with   -its own memory

it speaks   without consideration
for the burden most carry   when most

the yoked-   are wont to forget
asleep with   the density of our age

cursory partitions-   -against which I lean
tarried in grass-   to be torn inpart

the agonist wakes-   a whole of fragments
soundly separated   but bound to its host

when last he is-   -left to consider
what love is not   first and finally madness

on what is left is   a map of the universe

waiting and forgetting-   -again to be

possessed   the agonist wakes

soundly separated   a whole of fragments

there is-   -memory
in the mouth of the jackal   whole and

closed a house entirely-   -lossbegotten
I wake-   -in the queen s chamber

to my cat rasping over my ear   its tongue
I reach for my heart-   -in its black jar

and realize- -it is not too young to govern
that I am equidistant from two hard stars

listening   for the reliefs of the river delta
in the peasantine clacking of a wide loom

I dream of red   -roses in snow
this way   carmelina let s go

                              my blue heart   dreams for bread of breath
                              as deep   as your learned glide lingers

this way with me-   -come sing and know
until the eye of my eye--clouds with snow

                              as long as   your song lean fingers
                              make small-   -the sum of my blue being

I dream of red   -lips round in snow
that softly speaks and-   with late heat

                              my blue heart-   dreams like dance your
                              you- -knowing grin you glance your look

pressed against   the red moon hung low
my moon hung low   -red lips lift slow

                              started again   drawing open my door
                              to fill with soft pause   my blue four

you walked in-   on me
listening to channel orange-   -seated

sunning in the window- -whose wet light
sat like mustard-   on my skin

in my stomach   -like forget it s not
purple rain but   the walls you remember

me to   -they were orange and choked the
inside of a dream   -epileptic with stitches

two castles settled on-   the same seam of
selvage denim   that

would lay raw claim to my   name without
knowing and gnawing-   -at my ankle

you grab my shoulder-   also like a thing
to be thrown in bag -the gift I had hidden

behind my back   the game itself was all
the gift-   -but you weren t listening

the walls-   -you remember me to
they were orange and   the days passed

like the cooler side of a   -dream
sicle scyth   -ing the legs to letters

lame before   you touch me
now   -here

I ve been looking for you   my heart
for a long time   has been blue for you

I sat there-   -watching
in a small ravine   -an egret glean

a dead mouse   -in efforts to swallow it
in whole finally-   -tossing it its head

back- to catch the large body in its gullet-
a limp mass   passing like adam

behind its black lore-   -down
into its long white neck   in the shadow

of a newt   crawling on a ledge
above the ravine   -blotting the sun

from the mass in its craw   arced low
and stalking-   -to where the men

on calle tauro   walk in slow queue

but you were   -malnourished

I watched   wending its way
a robin singing-   -it settled

on the edge of a black fence-   -while
the sun came down gold against-   -the

glass and slid until red into the   evening
glow when its silent   fallen song

for what made it all so red   fell softly
and still warm-   -disappeared til morning

Andrew E. Colarusso is author of *The Sovereign* (Dalkey Archive, 2017),

Creance; or, Comest Thou Cosmic Nazarite (Northwestern University Press, 2018),

and *Souvenirs* (with Karen An-hwei Lee; Baobab Press, 2022).